Father to Son

Father to Son

Life Lessons on Raising a Boy

by Harry H. Harrison, Jr.

Workman Publishing Company

New York

The Cataloging-in-Publication Data for this book may be obtained from the Library of Congress.

ISBN-13: 978-0-7611-5072-5

Workman books are available at special discounts when purchased in bulk for

premiums and sales promotions as well as for fund-raising or educational use. Special

editions or book excerpts can be created to specification. For details, contact the

Special Sales Director at the address below.

Workman Publishing Company, Inc.

225 Varick Street

New York, NY 10014-4381

www.workman.com

Cover and book design by Paul Gamarello

Illustrations by Matt Wawiorka

Cover photograph by Julie Gang

Printed in Singapore

First printing April 2000

10 9 8 7 6 5 4 3 2 1

Sage and Field taught me everything I know.
Melissa made it all possible.

The Five Keys

Turning a boy into a man is a man's job. Since the beginning of time, it's been up to a father to make his son responsible. Kind. Courageous. Honorable.

A young boy doesn't come with instructions. He just comes with boundless love and an adventurous spirit. But the journey to manhood begins very early . . . the first time he looks at his dad and thinks, "I want to be like him."

·1·

Be around.

·2·

Be his father, not his friend. If you don't understand the difference, imagine his confusion when you must discipline him.

•3•

Be a good husband. Show his mom respect at all times.

·4·

Be home for dinner.

•5•

Be his hero.

Little Boys

Treasure your time
with your son.

Teach him to keep a secret.

Show him how to eat an Oreo. This is a skill that will serve him his entire life.

Set a strict bedtime as he's growing up. Boys need their sleep.

Teach him that he's
never too old to take
a nap.

Take him for walks and introduce him to the world of bugs.

Read to him nightly. He'll love it.

Don't let him sleep in your bed, even if he's scared or sick. Sleep in his room on the floor.

Make an effort to give up drinking and smoking. If he never sees his dad drinking, it will hold less mystery for him.

Teach him how to plant a flower.
It involves three things boys love—
dirt, digging, and water hoses.

Teach him to ride a two-wheel bike. It means freedom. Jog alongside.

Accept the fact he just might play with dolls. It's no big deal.

Ask him what he did today. Listen.

Take him to an amusement park. Ride the rides his mom wouldn't think of getting on. (At some point, of course, neither will you, so strike while the heart is healthy.)

Encourage the joy
of learning.

Teach him how to dial 911 and when and why.

Buy him something to hang from—a jungle gym or parallel bars. Something.

Show him how to throw a punch. Then raise him to never start a fight. And teach him to walk away.

Take him on hikes and show him how to ford a stream. Let him get wet and dirty.

Display his artwork in your office. Even that weird ashtray thing.

Let him hang out with you.
Remember, he has a need to be
around you, to learn what being
a man is all about.

An unhappy boy is often one who is hungry or tired. Or both.

Turn off the TV,
turn off the lights,
give him a flashlight,
and make up stories at night.
He won't be able to get enough.

Meet him for lunch at his school. Talk to him about what he's learned.

Talk to him about drugs and alcohol early, from about five years old and up. Because if you don't somebody else will.

Eat breakfast with him.

Show him how to clean his room. Little boys don't just learn this by osmosis.

If you buy him
Superman pajamas,
count on him launching himself
off counters, chairs, bunk beds—
and sometimes onto you.

Show him how to call you at work. Then take his calls. Forever.

Teach him magic.

Teach him not to litter.

Remind him often
to put the seat up.
Then to put the seat down.
Then to flush.

Teach him to throw up in the toilet, not on your bed. Many boys will stagger past two bathrooms just to destroy your bedroom.

Teach him to return
what he borrows.

Let him learn the joys of chocolate-chip cookie dough.

Reassure him he won't die if he spills a little blood.

Take your son to work with you every now and then. Pay as much attention to him as you do other people in the office.

Tell him sometimes you're wrong.

Race him. You'll never forget the day he beats you.

Give him responsibility.

Don't let the TV be a baby-sitter.

Make sure he knows
he's always safe at home.

Buy him a pet only when he's ready to take care of it. It will teach him to care about something besides himself.

Praise him often.

Teach him to compliment others.

Don't tolerate temper tantrums. Not now. Not when he's 15. The world won't.

Scream at him and you will raise a screamer.

Teach him not to hurt others.

Don't let him quit out of frustration. He won't learn anything.

His favorite game for a long,
long time will be playing with you.
Be available.
Even when you're tired. Even
when the presentation went south.
Be available.

Encourage him to go barefoot.

Teach him to lock his bike.

Teach him not to be afraid
of animals, but to respect them.

Ask him who his heroes are. These are the people he'll copy.

Talk to him about what he wants to be when he grows up. Don't be alarmed by his answer.

Teach him the wonder of staring at the moon.

Teach him that every life
is precious.

Help him to understand that his word is his bond. And remember, he'll learn from you.

Teach him that if he waters grass, it will grow.

Help him bury his pet.

Remember, little boys love their grandfathers. No one really knows why.

Without scaring him, talk to him about bad people and what he should do when they approach.

Insist he play outside a lot. It's much healthier than watching TV or playing computer games.

Show him how to do
a wheelie.

Never forget that you can't hug or cuddle or kiss a young boy too much.

Remember, boys are like lion cubs: They show their affection by hugging, wrestling, and rolling around on top of each other.

Don't fight his fights.

Never tell him boys don't cry. Ask him why he's crying.

Teach him to clean up his own mess.

Allow him to believe in
Santa Claus.
And the Easter Bunny.
And the Tooth Fairy.
Promote the sense of wonder.
He'll never stop looking for it.

Leave the office early to play with him.

Teach him to share.

Give him piano lessons.

Realize there are some things you can't teach him.

Let him watch you shave. This is where he begins to put two and two together.

Teach him to respect authority,
but not to be in awe of it.

Encourage him to make friends with the white boy, the black boy, and the Chinese kid who doesn't speak a word of English.

If you spend time with him and his friends when he's young, he won't think twice about you being around his friends when he's older.

Teach him the joys of peanut butter and honey.

Show him how
to tie a tie and how to
polish his shoes.

Remember—the values you teach him now he'll have as a teenager.

Check his homework nightly. Don't leave this totally up to his mom. He'll see how important his studying is to you.

Even if you can, don't buy him everything.

Remember, bullying him is a guaranteed way to raise a bully.

Teach him how to find
his way home.

Don't criticize his mistakes. Criticize his lack of effort.

Teach him to spit.
He'll practice all day.

Take him for doughnuts Saturday morning. Let his mom sleep late.

Teach him how to use a computer. How to type. How to send e-mail.

Share a big plate of ribs.
The messier the better.

Teach him never to be afraid to try new things.

Boys & Sports

Don't forget that
the point of sports when
you're a kid
is to have fun.

Realize that while he's young, one of your son's favorite things about organized sports is the uniform. Let him wear it to school.

Try not to miss his games.
A boy loves playing in front of
his dad and hearing him cheer.
He'll always ask,
"Did you see me?"

Celebrate after every game.

Show him how to put a baseball in a new glove and wrap a belt around it.

Teach him how to throw a curve.

Take him fishing.

Take him to the golf course
and teach him to play.
Even if he's three.
Be patient.

Remember that little boys get distracted by bugs and dirt and lots of other stuff even while a game is happening all around them. Yelling will not change this.

If you find yourself yelling at him or the referee, take a book to the games and go sit far away from everyone else. They'll think you're a bit odd, but your son will appreciate it.

If his coach is a screamer, find another team. If you're the coach, retire.

Teach him to swim.
If you don't know how,
get him lessons.

Show him how to lift weights.

Take him to hockey games. Boys love the fights. (Totally politically incorrect, but a fact.)

Make him carry his own athletic bag.

Take him horseback riding.
(It could be a 15-year-old three-legged mare and he'll remember
a white stallion.)

Do not criticize him after his games. He knows exactly what he did. He needs a father to support him. His coach will criticize him.

Practice with him and he will get better. This goes for anything . . . including math.

Don't think he'll turn pro because he scores more often than other kids. On the other hand, don't think he's destined for a life of geekdom just because he's the worst player on the team. Either way, the odds are he will be exactly average by the time he's seventeen.

Read the sports section
with him.
(Reading is reading.)

Keep in mind, if his soccer (or baseball or basketball or any game) team is more important to you than it is to him, something is wrong.
With you.

Teach him how to lose.

Teach him how to win.

Do not tolerate bad sportsmanship in him. If you do, it will stay with him the rest of his life.

Tell him "no pass, no play." Even if he misses the regional soccer playoff.

Teach him that just because he isn't the best, doesn't mean he can't enjoy it.

Accept the fact
he may not be a quarterback,
he may be a tuba player.
And a fine one at that.

Boys &
Spirituality

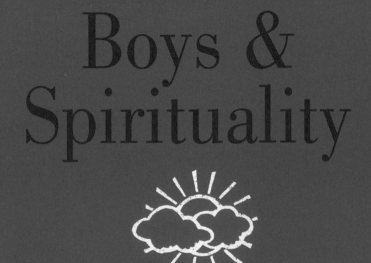

Remember, your primary duty as a father is to develop your son's spiritual well-being.

Teach him the difference between being lonely and being alone.

Teach him that success in the face of adversity is the greatest success of all.

Teach him that self-esteem can only be achieved by achieving.

Talk to him about God, about Jesus, about Moses, about spiritual leaders often. Start this when he's young and he won't be shy talking about them as a teenager.

Remember, if you can't talk to your son about God, then you've never really talked to him.

Take him to Sunday school or Hebrew school or religious school regularly. He'll say he doesn't like it. But one day you'll notice you have an outstanding teenager who still says he doesn't like religious school.

Pray together as a family, then teach him to pray on his own.

When he's confronted with a serious problem, encourage him to ask God for help in solving it.

Teach him that God answers every prayer. Sometimes with a no.

Teach him God can
be trusted.

Teach him to pray for his enemies.

Teach him to believe that
as he gives to the world,
so the world
will give back to him.

Teach him to give anonymously.

Teach him to treat each day as holy.

Show him how to meditate.

Teach him that self-pity
is a waste of time.

Be prepared for him to come home one day a complete agnostic.

Teach him that forgiving someone isn't a weakness, but the height of selfishness—because it makes you feel so much better.

Boys & Money

Give your son an allowance based on his age and the chores he performs. Realize he'll always want more.

Teach him how to
negotiate a raise.

Buy him a wallet.

Teach him nothing is free.

Never be afraid to say,
"We can't afford it."

Teach him that if he wants something bad enough, that is a reason to go to work.

If he needs it, loan him money. Make him pay you back.

Teach him to save.
Help him open a
savings account.

Teach him to wait
for sales.

A young boy loses things.
A teen who loses things
and then does without
learns not to lose things.

Teach him that you don't have to spend a lot for a good haircut.

Teach him that
if he can't buy the best,
buy the best value.

Help him buy a small amount of stock with his own money when he's twelve. Think how rich he'll be if he keeps that up for fifty years.

Teach him to pay his bills promptly.

Teach him how to read a financial page. If you don't know how, learn with him.

Insist he get a job by fifteen. The fact he doesn't like it is the last reason not to do it.

Show him how to write a check and balance a checkbook. He'll say he knows how, but he really doesn't.

Teach him not to make a
bet that he can't pay.

Show him how to return something to the store and get his money back.

Teach him to use a credit card only in emergencies, then give him one.

Teach him to never pay list price for an automobile.

Boys & Girls

Let your son know you're as confused about women as he is.

Be sure to meet his girlfriends.

Remind him that it doesn't matter if she doesn't have a curfew. He does.

Treat his girlfriends with respect. Make sure he does.

Don't embarrass him when it comes to girls, although often your just being alive will be embarrassing enough. Still, when he goes to parties, have no qualms about calling to see if the parents are going to be home.

When you drive him on dates, make sure he gets out of the car to get his girlfriend. You'd be amazed how many boys still think they can just honk and she'll come running.

Do not read the notes that he puts in his desk.

Talk to him frankly about sex.
And your expectations of him.

Hug and kiss his mother in front of him often. He'll say he's disgusted, but ignore him.

Never criticize his mother in front of him. Never, never, never.

Teach him to compliment his mother's cooking. Even when it's liver and onions.

Realize you can't mend
his broken heart.
You can comfort it, however.

Encourage him to ask out that blonde.

Older Boys

Remember that older boys don't have "baby" sitters.

Teach him to set goals. Start small. For many teenage boys, just setting the alarm clock is a goal.

Teach him to wash and fold his laundry.

Remind him that school isn't a place for self-expression. It's a place for learning.

Show him your high school yearbook so that both of you will know how goofy you once looked.

Drive him and his friends to the movies. It's a way of learning who his friends are.

Let him earn your respect.

Talk to him about his dreams.
And about yours.

Let him fail.

Teach him that he can learn as much from failure as he can from success.

Teach him that there's a direct correlation between studying and good grades.

Teach him that most everything
is okay in moderation.
Including moderation.

Listen to him when he talks—all evening, if that's what he wants.

Remember, he's watching how you treat your dad.

Give him responsibility.
It separates boys
from men.

Don't defend his stupid actions. He'll learn he can get away with stupidity. Hold him accountable.

Teach him a respect
for books.

Teach him how to barbecue a steak. This is a rite of passage.

Make him laugh. Trade jokes.

Hug him before bedtime
every night.
Even when he's eighteen.

Tell him often that you love him.

Make sure he spends time around his aunts and uncles, cousins and grandparents. He may not like all of them, but he'll develop a love for family.

Teach him to channel his anger.

Teach him that the only way to conquer fear is to walk through it.

Remind him often that he's capable of changing the world.

Teach him tolerance.

When he's done something wrong, confront him immediately. Don't worry about hurting his feelings, but after you've chewed him out, it's time for you to get over it.

Don't hold a grudge against him.

Teach him the value
of wisdom.

Unfailingly, be kind.

Try not to criticize him in front of his friends.

Make sure his friends know that alcohol and drugs are not welcome in your house.

Put a computer in his room. Never a TV.

Let him buy his own stereo.
Don't be alarmed at his music.
Remember, your music terrified
your parents.

Don't adjust the house to his moods. Let him adjust to yours.

Teach him to be on time and to call if he's going to be late. Always.

Teach him the secret to solving even the most complicated problems is to just begin.

I f you've taught him not to get in a car driven by a drunk, he won't.

Teach him to wear a
seat belt.

Talk to him often about college.

At dinner, talk about politics, science, religion, what he did in school that day.

Sometimes you will just have to talk to your son about things that will upset him: friends using drugs, his behavior, and so on. This is where a father earns his money.

Raise him not to tolerate alcohol or drugs at his parties, and to refuse them if offered at others' parties. Tell him this does not mean he's a loser. It just means he's smart.

Don't dismiss any dream of his as too big.

Teach him that jealousy serves no purpose but to make you feel bad.

Teach him what is important in life—and it's not a car or a stereo or any "thing."

Allow him to wear your clothes, your shoes, your socks as soon as they fit him. This is okay. When you can no longer find any of your clothes, start borrowing his.

Teach him that no possession is worth stealing.

Teach him there are times to stay between the lines. Like on highways.

Teach him to roll his car windows up at night and lock his car.

Teach him to give things away.

Teach him that men do clean up the kitchen and the house. Every day.

Until he graduates, set curfews and stick to them. When he's a senior, make a more lenient curfew conditional upon his grades.

Encourage him to participate in some kind of community service. This is where giving back begins.

Teach him to buy his mother holiday gifts and Mother's Day cards—and with his own money as he gets older.

Encourage him to run for student government.

Teach him how to look someone in the eye and to shake hands firmly.

Let him face the consequences
of his own actions.
They are the best teachers.

Teach him patience,
kindness, and tolerance.
If you don't,
many years from now
you'll wish you had.

Teach him nothing that he ever does—or is going to do—is worth lying to you about.

Expect excellence.

Teach him to stand up for what's right, even when everyone else thinks he's wrong.
Even you.

Teach him that every action has a consequence.

Never, ever permit him to talk back—to you or to his mother. This will teach him to respect you . . . as well as other adults, like his teachers.

Monitor the movies and TV he watches. This may mean you have to monitor what you watch, too.

Be prepared to answer
difficult questions
without editorial
comment.

Teach him how to drive. How to drive downtown. How to drive in the rain. How to drive in the snow.

Condition his use of the car upon his grades. He'll become an Einstein.

Show him how to pump gas and check his tires. (You would think he knows, but he doesn't.)

Lay down strict laws about drinking and driving. Enforce them religiously. If he does wind up in traffic court (and he might), make sure he dresses nicely. This will teach him that to get along in the adult world, he has to look and act like one.

If he's guilty, do not take his side. He deserves what he's about to get. This could be an opportune time for him to learn about apologies and being cool under pressure.

If he does come in smelling of alcohol, throw the book at him. But that's the only thing.

If he cheats and gets caught,
let him suffer the consequences.
At school and at home.

Teach him to floss.

Buy him deodorant and the whole house will smell better.

Show him how to shave with a safety razor and how to wad up little tissues to stem the blood. This could save him a fortune in bloodstained shirts.

Don't get freaked out over long hair. Draw the line at stupid hair.

Know the difference between normal teen behavior and questionable teen behavior. Learn to accept and live with your normal teen.

Teach him that trust is like fine china. Once it's broken, it takes a while to put it back together.

Don't issue an
ultimatum you can't
live with.

Hang a punching bag in the garage . . . it absorbs a lot of sibling rivalry.

Teach him to stand up straight.

Teach him that there's honor in even a minimum-wage job. And money.

Tell him to call his boss if he's going to miss work or be late.

Believe in him.

Remember, teenage boys like looking at themselves in the mirror. Every now and then ask him what he thinks he sees.

Do push-ups together.

Show him how to gargle. If you don't, your bathroom could be irreparably harmed.

Realize that you can't be everything to him.

Teach him the joy of finishing a job.

Teach him that the world will judge him by his actions, not his intentions.

Remind him to be on time. The world doesn't operate on teenage time.

Don't tolerate his moodiness, and you won't have moods to tolerate.

Teach him that rules,
even dumb rules,
shouldn't be broken.

Make time to be alone with him.

Teach him how to apologize.
Saying "Sorry" is not
the same as saying
"I'm sorry."

Tell him to chew with his mouth closed and talk with it open.

Show him how to eat with chopsticks. As well as a knife and fork.

If you go on a business trip, call him. He misses you.

Show him how to change a tire. If you don't know how, get someone to teach you both.

Teach him that reckless people usually end up doing more damage to others than to themselves.

Teach him that true independence means he pays.

Assure him that having a clean room doesn't make him a nerd. It just means he can find his underwear.

Encourage him to trust
his instincts.
If something feels unsafe,
it probably is.

Realize that if you do something once, he might think of it as a tradition. (Boys are really weird that way.)

If he's been up late at night and sleeps past noon, wake him up and give him something to do.

Teach him that the only constant thing in life is change.

Teach him not to judge
a book by its cover.

Teach him to read the
instructions.

Teach him that it's possible to work too hard.

Teach him that the solution to most problems isn't a pill.

Teach him that there's no harm
in failure, but in the failure to try.

Teach him how to use a hammer, a screwdriver, and a saw.

Teach him not to burn bridges.

Teach him to treasure
his friends.

Teach him to ask for help.

Show him how to read
a map.

Teach him to be kind.

Teach him that he's in charge of his own destiny.

Teach him that there is nothing to fear but fear itself.

Teach him how to iron.

Teach him not to hold on to anything too tightly.

Teach him that appearances do matter.

Teach him to reach for the stars.

Promise you'll always be there for him.

Tell him to never give up.

Teach him to call
his mom.

In the end,

Let him go.